APARTMENTS DESIGNSOURCE

APARTMENTS DESIGNSOURCE

COLLINS | **DESIGN**

An Imprint of HarperCollinsPublishers

HarperCollins books may be purchased for educational, business, or sales promotional use.
For information, please write: Special Markets Department, HarperCollins Publishers,
10 East 53rd Street, New York, NY 10022

First Edition published in 2006 by:
Collins Design
An Imprint of HarperCollins*Publishers*
10 East 53rd Street
New York, NY 10022
Tel.: (212) 207-7000
Fax: (212) 207-7654
collinsdesign@harpercollins.com
www.harpercollins.com

Distributed throughout the world by:
HarperCollins*Publishers*
10 East 53rd Street
New York, NY 10022
Fax: (212) 207-7654

Packaged by
LOFT Publications
Via Laietana, 32 4.° Of. 92
08003 Barcelona, Spain
Tel.: +34 932 688 088
Fax: +34 932 687 073
loft@loftpublications.com
www.loftpublications.com

Editor:
Ana G. Cañizares

Art Director:
Mireia Casanovas Soley

Layout:
Cristina Granero Navarro

Library of Congress Cataloging-in-Publication Data

Cañizares, Ana Cristina G.
 Apartments designsource / Ana G. Cañizares.—1st ed.
    p. cm.
 ISBN-13: 978-0-06-084715-9 (paperback with flaps)
 ISBN-10: 0-06-084715-8 (paperback with flaps)
 1. Apartments. 2. Interior decoration. 3. Interior architecture.
 I. Title: Apartments design source. II. Title.
 NK2195.A6D35 2006
 747'.88314—dc22

                                        2005031532

Second Printing, 2006

Contents_

The apartment is the sacred place of the urbanite, a sheltered haven, an oasis in the midst of chaos, a multipurpose space that offers the possibility of private life and coexistence with others. The existence and persisting growth of the city has rendered the apartment a necessary and practical typology in bustling metropolises around the world. A dose of design know-how offers the possibility of transforming this cherished space into a truly unique, contemporary, and dynamic living area.

As part of the DesignSource series, this book presents a selection of apartments that aims to serve as a source of inspiration to the average homeowner and architect alike in search of ideas for how to design or improve their own apartment space. The manipulation of light, surface area, and ceiling height, combined with an appropriate choice of materials and use of colors and textures can transform a dull and inanimate space into a luminous, spacious, and attractive interior. By introducing multifunctional furnishings and layouts, an apartment can also easily incorporate an office or studio space from which to work or provide for all the necessary domestic functions within a very limited surface area.

The wide variety of apartments shown here display an ample range of design solutions that suit an extensive number of apartment types, from single-room studios to loft-style residences. Featuring the work of designers and architects from around the world, the selection takes the reader on a visual journey through stunning private interiors located in the world's major capitals, exhibiting the latest trends in international contemporary design.

Flex House_Archikubik

© Eugeni Pons/Barcelona, Spain

□ The architect of this loft-style apartment divided the space into a day zone and a night zone separated by the structural element that contains the bathroom. This solution provides the sensation of open space and allows the wooden-beam ceiling to remain exposed.

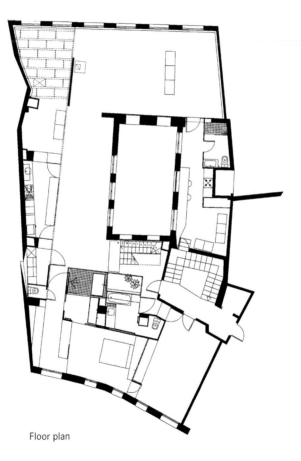

Floor plan

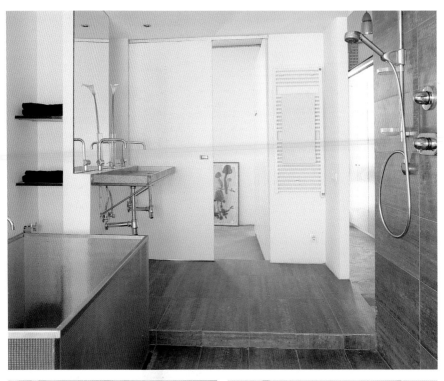

☐ Loft in an Attic_Manuel Ocaña del Valle

© Luis Asín / Madrid, Spain

□ Located in a 150-year-old building in the Madrid neighborhood of Chueca, the loft provides for many uses resolved in unitary and flexible spaces. A folding glass door divides the space into two parts. A closet is located under the staircase, and the kitchen and bathroom on the ground floor are grouped together so the rest of the space can remain open.

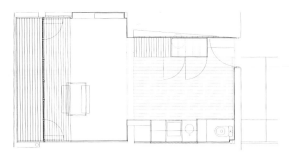

Ground floor plan

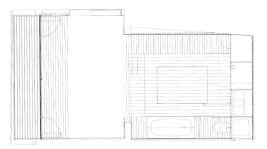

Attic floor plan

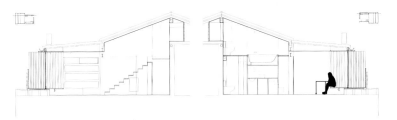

Longitudinal sections

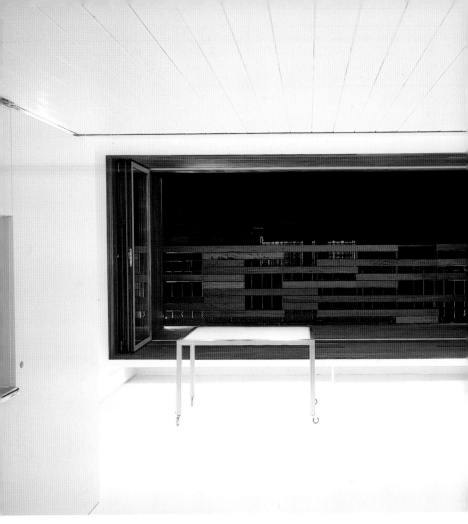

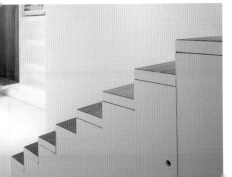

□ Starting with the wooden box on the terrace, everything was painted white in order to instill the space with a sense of calm and to amplify the feeling of spaciousness. The furnishings, also in white, emphasize this theme and merge with the interior architecture.

☐ In the attic, the loft is separated from the bedroom by a matted, white glass screen that does not reach the ceiling or floor. This gives the space the same flexibility and amplitude as the rest of the apartment.

Michigan Avenue Apartment_Pablo Uribe

© Pep Escoda/Miami, FL, United States

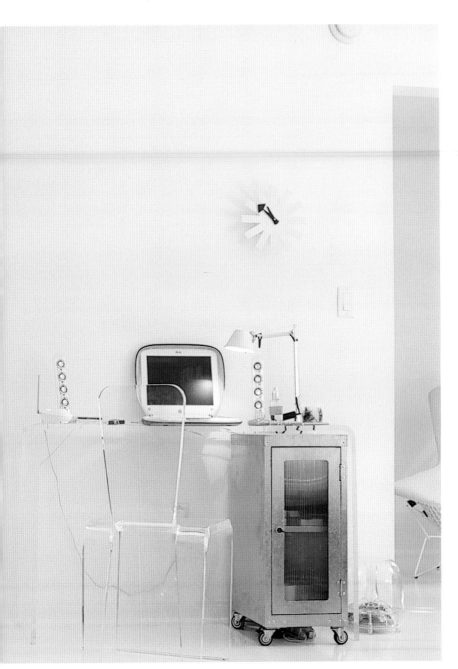

☐ This efficient, square-shaped apartment is on the second floor of a 1951 building in the heart of Miami Beach. The space is composed of four principal units: the living room/bedroom/dining room, the study/kitchen, the corridor, and the bathroom. The view of the interior garden that it shares with the rest of the complex adds to the feeling of spaciousness.

☐ The original wood floor was painted white to highlight the contemporary look while enhancing the feeling of spaciousness and playing with the "endless" effect used in photography studios. The furniture was chosen to make the best use of the limited space, creating a series of multifunctional areas—hence the idea of an opium bed as a central feature.

Olympic Tower Residence_Gabellini Associates

© Paul Warchol/New York, NY, United States

☐ The design concept of this luxury
apartment located on New York's
Fifth Avenue consists of a light,
crystal-clear space that functions as
an observatory of the metropolitan
collage. The atmosphere of the
interior is created with high-quality
materials and a palette dominated
by white plaster, marble from
Yugoslavia, and translucent crystal.

Floor plan

Apartment on Flinders Lane_Staughton Architects

© Shannon McGrath/Melbourne, Australia

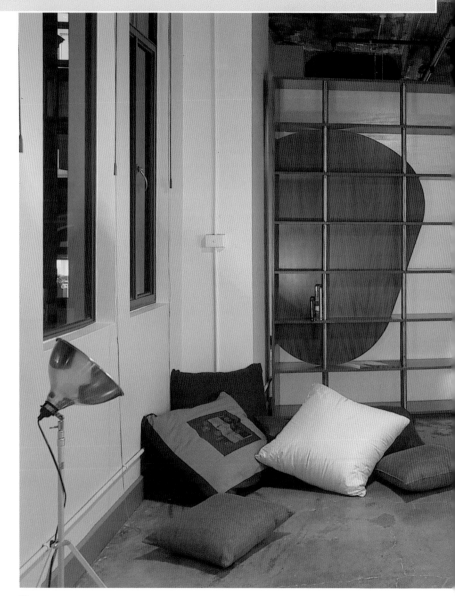

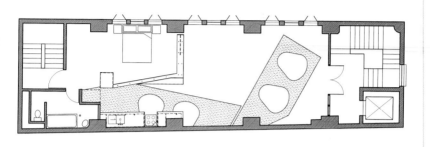

Floor plan

☐ This space is located in an old office building that was converted to an apartment complex in the heart of Melbourne, Australia. The project is primarily defined by a multifunctional, free-standing wood-framed unit that encloses the sleeping area, provides storage space, serves as an auxiliary dining room, includes bookshelves, and is a sculptural element in and of itself.

Apartment on Ocean Drive_Dd Allen

© Pep Escoda/Miami, FL, United States

☐ This apartment is situated on the top floor of an early 1960s building typical of the area. Most of the design and decorative work consisted in the search for elements characteristic of this architectural style. To create a sense of spaciousness, the dividing wall was removed, leaving a single open space marked by a structural reinforced-concrete column.

☐ Smith Apartment_Smart Design Studio

© Sharrin Rees / Sydney, Australia

□ A three-bedroom apartment was turned into a two-bedroom home complemented by a studio that doubles as a guest bedroom. The decorative details are modern and the materials unobtrusive, allowing the art collection and the spectacular views of the city to capture the attention.

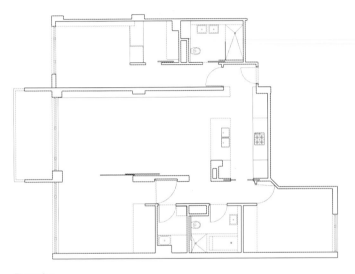

Floor plan

☐ The steel-framed glass panels,
the work of the artist Janet
Lawrence, offer a practical means of
separating or uniting the studio and
the sitting room. It combines with
the other artworks to create a
comfortable, peaceful atmosphere,
thereby attaining a perfect marriage
of simplicity and stylishness.

London Mews Conversion_Co-labarchitects

© Mat Jessop/London, United Kingdom

☐ The client for this project wished to create a private residence by combining two typical commercial mews in London. Several skylights and mirrors were introduced to enhance light and the sensation of space, while the rich color and texture of the materials create a soft, warm atmosphere appropriate for the new residential function.

Ground floor

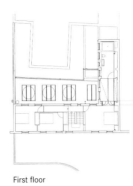

First floor

Sections

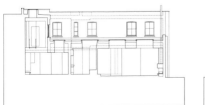

Elevations

Everything in a Cabinet_Guillaume Terver & Fabienne Couvert

© Guillaume Terver & Fabienne Couvert/Paris, France

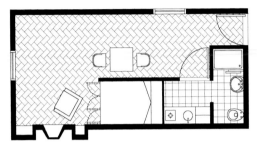

Floor plan

□ This 322-square-foot studio makes use of innovative technical and functional solutions that are grouped into a single object: a cabinet. All the various components of the residence are contained in the box: the bed in the upper part, a door underneath that leads to the kitchen, a closet at the end, and a glass space for the television.

Apartment on Rue Rochechouart_Peter Tyberghien

© Alejandro Bahamón/Paris, France

☐ This compact and luxurious apartment was created for the purpose of receiving guests during short stays in the city of Paris. A unique layout features a liquid-crystal partition that switches from transparent to frosted at the touch of a button, separating the bed from the bathtub.

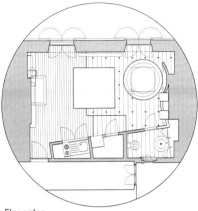

Floor plan

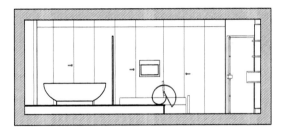

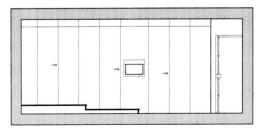

Sections

☐ A series of folding doors hides a small kitchen, closet, and half-bath, which is the only independent element inside the apartment. The finishes and furnishings are replete with details that define the project and make this apartment a sophisticated, comfortable, and relaxing place.

☐ Basic and Functional_Christopher Ash & James Soane

☐ The idea behind the design of this apartment was to provide all of the spaces with natural light, while dividing the bedroom area from the living zones and conferring on them very different spatial characters. The arrangement makes the most of the generous light from the windows while creating diverse settings without the need for divisions inside the space.

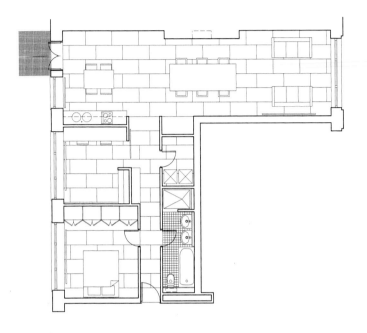

Floor plan

The hallway ends at a large
common space, which combines the
living room, the dining room, and the
kitchen into one environment with
ample proportions. In order to give
the space the character of a
traditional residence, a part of the
kitchen was extended toward a small
terrace that had previously been
used as an emergency exit.

Sempacher Apartments_Camenzind Evolution

© Camenzind Evolution/Zurich, Switzerland

The Sempacher building, located in a residential area of Zurich, is an example of modern and sustainable urban restoration. The project incorporates a flexible structure that allows future generations to make changes, maintains a harmonious dialogue with the surrounding structures, and remains sensitive to its environment, taking into account the life cycles of its materials.

□ The interior spaces have a utility core, where the kitchens and bathrooms are located, allowing the living quarters to be more flexible.

Ground floor   First floor   Second floor

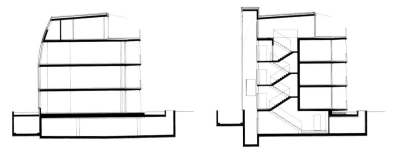

Sections

Spatial Relations_McDonnell Associates

© Carlos Domínguez/London, United Kingdom

□ This project's main challenge was to allow for mobility so that the lighting or the structure of the interior spaces could be easily altered. The solutions include curtains that diffuse the light; a pivoting, horizontal door that separates the kitchen from the dining room; and another vertical door that separates the living room from the staircase.

A Continual Path_Luis Cuartas & Guillermo Arias

© Eduardo Consuegra/Bogotá, Colombia

☐ This project forms part of an integral reformation that the two architects carried out on an old building in the center of Bogotá. The goal was to create a continuous space with diverse relationships between the different areas and a circular, continuous path that traverses the entire residence.

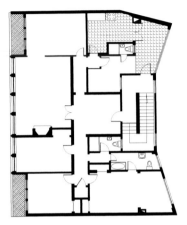

Previous floor distribution

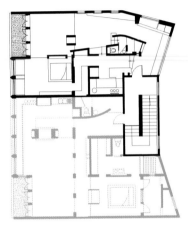

Present floor distribution

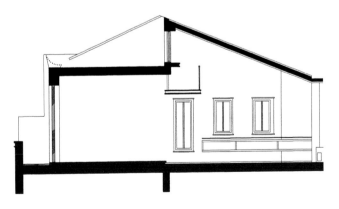

Transversal section

Apartment in Berlin_Abcarius & Burns Architecture Design

© Ludger Paffrath/Berlin, Germany

□ Situated inside a new apartment building in the historic center of Berlin, this apartment explores new ways of integrating the conventional functions of a traditional household. Composed of various parallel volumes that channel light into the space, the apartment incorporates mobile panels that enable its transformation into different configurations.

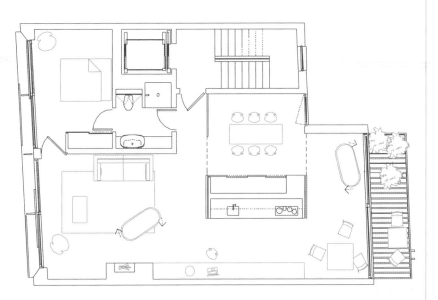

Floor plan

Apartment in Parque España_Ten Arquitectos

© Jaime Navarro / Mexico DF, Mexico

□ This apartment is one of the six contained within the entire building, which also houses a contemporary art gallery and ground-floor parking. Each apartment, which occupies an entire floor, boasts an open-plan space in which the tenants can organize the living areas any way they desire.

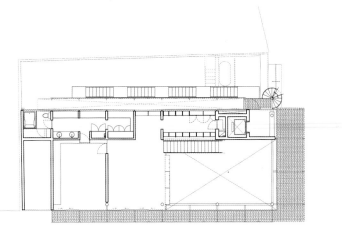

Penthouse lower level

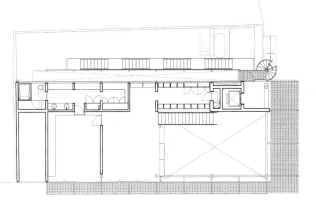

Penthouse upper level

☐ The rooms generally face the street and are protected by a narrow balcony made of aluminum. Double-height spaces, translucent sliding doors, and full-length windows are the characteristic elements of this spacious and luminous apartment.

Bishop's Mansions Apartment_Pablo Uribe

© Montse Garriga/London, United Kingdom

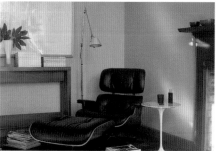

□ This apartment's exceptional location, on the ground floor of a house in Fulham, London, that dates back to 1900, makes for an especially peaceful setting. Although the renovation completely breaks with the original Victorian style, it employs materials that connect with that type of architecture, including the unfinished brick, dark wood, and light colors.

□ The architect eliminated all the nonstructural walls and created a series of connected areas, from the front yard to the rear garden, where household activities can take place in a single setting.

Apartment in Dornbirn_Geli Salzmann

© Ignacio Martínez/Dornbirn, Austria

☐ Originally a tavern and
blacksmith's stable, this space was
renovated into an apartment and
organized around two units of
furniture laid out parallel to the
entrance: the large table that serves
as the dining area and counter, and
the sideboard that marks off the
bathroom.

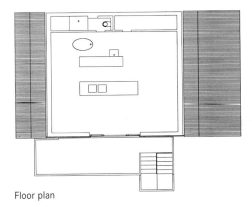

Floor plan

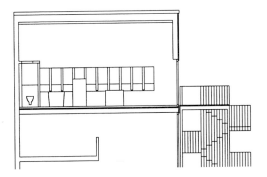

Longitudinal section

Transversal section

☐ Apartment in Milan_Luca Rolla

© Andrea Martiredonna/Milan, Italy

□ The architects for this project removed the existing partitions to leave a large open space; the idea was to create a more private night-time space between two daytime areas, the sitting-dining room and the studio. The masonry walls marking off the rooms do not reach the ceiling and contain openings that facilitate the circulation of air and the entrance of light.

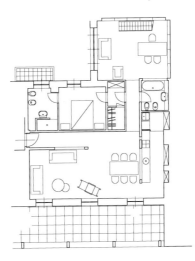

Plans

☐ The upper floor—a small garret with a guest bedroom—is reached through the studio. A wood-and-metal staircase rises between the bookcase and the table, but its modern lines and lightness make it an element that is both functional and decorative. The simple decoration in the studio stands out against the minimal furnishings and the teak parquet, which adds a touch of warmth.

☐ The masonry walls divide the various spaces in the daytime areas. One of them forms a corridor that leads to the living room, another separates the kitchen from the dining room, and a third one exists between the bathroom and the studio. The openings in these walls create a feeling of uniformity and continuity throughout the apartment.

Around Table_Smart Architects

© Gene Raymond Ross/Sydney, Australia

The layout of this apartment, located on Australia's famous Bondi Beach, is organized around a dining table that rotates 180 degrees in order to function as a surface for the kitchen, studio, or living room. This dynamic feature is an essential space saver ideal for small apartments, which allows for the transformation of a single space without having to add extra furnishings.

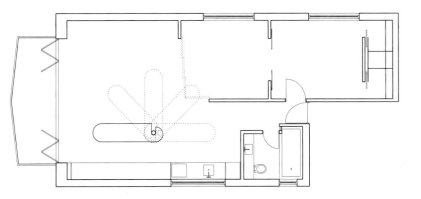

Floor plan

Glass Box_EoK – Eichinger oder Knechtl

© Margherita Spiluttini/Vienna, Austria

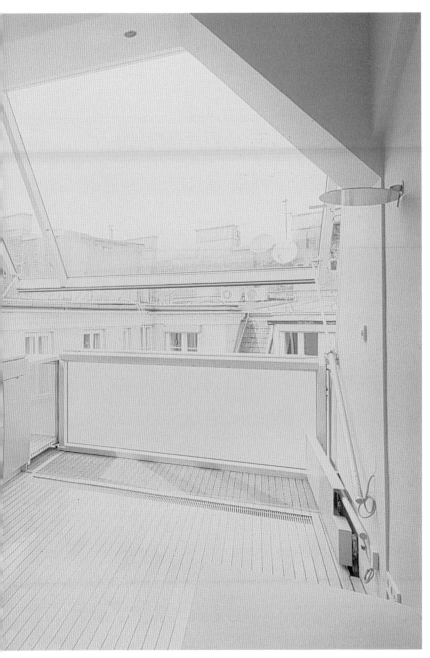

☐ An old laundry on the attic floor of a building was converted into a small, luminous apartment. Existing partitions were removed, ceiling beams were covered with sheet metal, and the exterior wall was replaced by a large folding glass window. Inside, a wire-mesh covering integrates cabinets and divides the different areas.

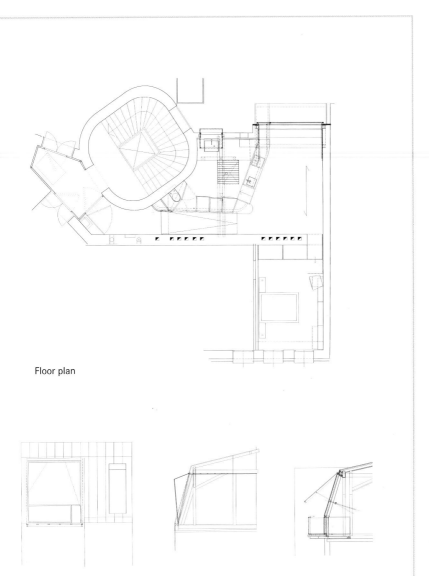

Floor plan

Details

] Translucent and reflective
materials are used to maximize
ght. A neutral palette consisting
f whites and grays and the light
ak wood floor laid in thin narrow
trips contribute to the atmosphere
f the apartment.

□ The apartment's primary feature, apart from its motorized glass façade, is its complex composition of curved corners and angled lines—which is echoed in the sparse furniture contained within this small glass box. The wire-mesh screen serves as a divider to partition off different spaces, such as the bathroom and shower.

Apartment in Lisbon_Inês Lobo

© Sergio Mah/Lisbon, Portugal

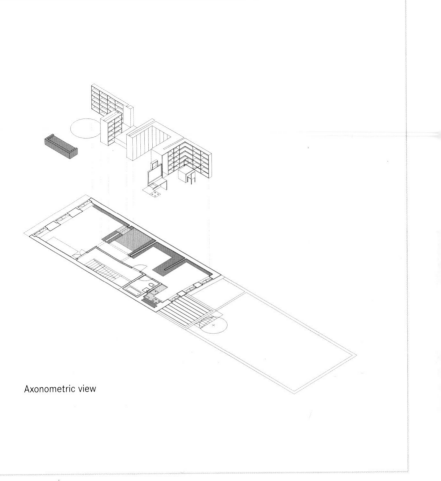

Axonometric view

☐ The striking design of this apartment, blending beautifully with the existing architecture, is based on simple, restrained lines. One continuous storage and shelving unit skirts the side of the apartment and the walls like a second skin covering the interior. This unit clearly divides the space into four rooms that accommodate the various living functions.

Flatiron District Loft_Donald Billinkoff Architects

© Elliott Kaufman Photography/New York, NY, United States

☐ Previously a photographic studio and apartment, this loft, located in the Flatiron District in the center of New York, was renovated and transformed into a family residence. Auxiliary spaces—the bedrooms, bathrooms, and the television room—are laid out around a large area that includes the living, dining, and play areas.

☐ The kitchen, adjacent to the main area, features a glass-brick wall that separates it from a public hallway in the building. This structure allows light to flow into the apartment, transforming it into a large-scale light fixture at night.

Previous plan

New plan

☐ **Roof under Roof**_Barbara de Vries & Alastair Gordon

© G. de Chabaneix/New Jersey, United States

The clients for this renovation wished to preserve certain elements and adapt them to their new home: the industrial style, the brick walls, the immense windows, the open ceiling, and the cement floor. The abandoned brick factory was transformed into a residence through the use of wooden sheets that create an intimate space inside the larger volume.

☐ Vintage elements retain the original character of the space.

Minimum and Austere_Sandra Aparicio & Ignacio Forteza

© Eugeni Pons/Barcelona, Spain

□ This project entailed designing an apartment that carefully incorporates the basic functions with minimal elements. Different atmospheres were created through the placement of the furniture. In the open space, with reduced dimensions, the designers separated the bedroom from the living room using a piece of furniture that contains the television and also serves as the dining table.

Floor plan

Light and Dark_Karin Léopold & François Fauconnet

© Vincent Leroux/ACI Roca-Sastre/Paris, France

☐ The architects' aim was to provide this apartment with all the elements that are indispensable for comfort without dividing the space. They organized the project around a cabinet in which they grouped the toilet, the heating system, shelves, and the entrance door, which became one more component of this innovative structure.

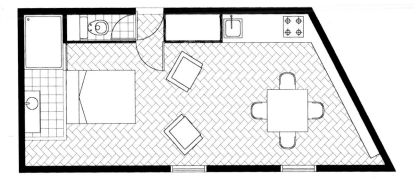

Floor plan

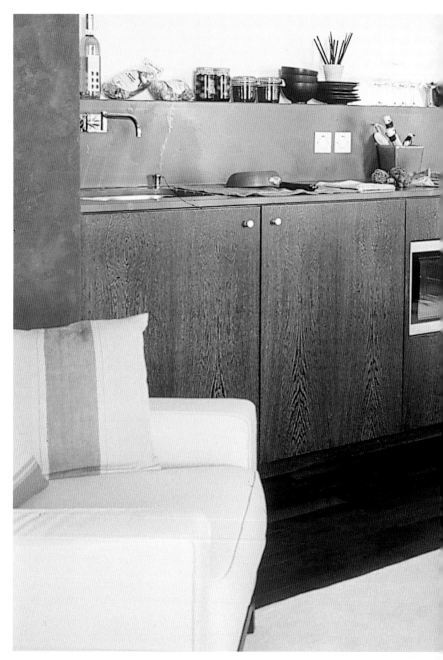

Functional Folds_Stéphane Chamard

© Vincent Leroux/ACI Roca-Sastre/Paris, France

□ The young architect, Stéphane Chamard, transformed this tiny surface area into a luminous interior in which to live and work. The area consists of a cubic space with high ceilings, which permitted the architect to create two floors. Chamard used every last inch, making the most of the room and its openings by giving them a functional character.

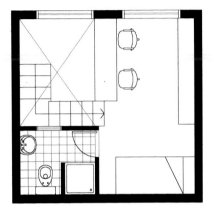

Upper floor plan

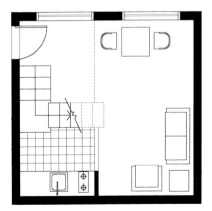

Ground floor plan

La Magdalena Apartment_Guillermo Arias

© Pablo Rojas & Álvaro Gutiérrez/Bogotá, Colombia

The plan for this project called for a fully integrated space, with the living area and bedroom located in what was originally the main living room. A white-painted wooden unit unobtrusively divides these two areas and does duty as a bookcase, television cabinet, and music center.

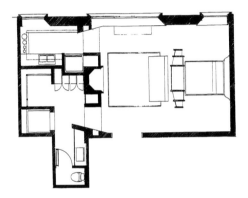

Floor plan

☐ In the living areas, bedroom, and
bath, the dominant color is white.
Many details, such as the molding
for the false ceiling and the lamps,
were designed by the architect
himself to preserve the original
character of the space.

☐ Mp3 Residence_Michel Rojkind & Simon Hamui

© Jaime Navarro/Mexico DF, Mexico

RE) SUPPOSED

□ Designed for a young actor
looking for a dynamic and sensual
residence, this previously cluttered
space was opened up and
redistributed, resulting in a spacious
and luminous apartment.
Throughout the two-and-a-half-
story volume, frosted glass panels
were introduced to separate the
different environments.

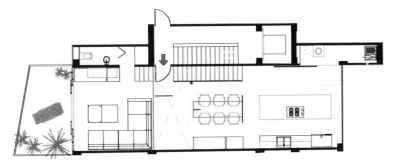

Lower level

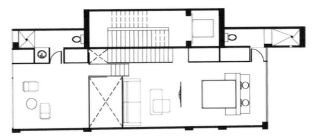

Upper level

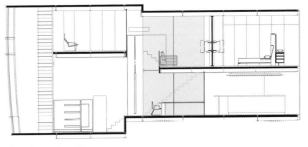

Longitudinal section

The distribution of functional
areas over open tiers increases the
sensation of space, visually links the
various areas, and creates a
dynamic relationship between the
dwelling and its occupant.

Two Atmospheres and a Box_Mónica Pla

© José Luis Haussman/Barcelona, Spain

☐ This deteriorated and neglected
space was transformed with the goal
of creating a luminous and spacious
residence within a single
environment. To separate the
bedroom from the main room and
still maintain spatial continuity,
designer Mónica Pla placed the
bathroom between these two
spaces. Accessible from the
bedroom, the bathroom includes a
shower and is situated in a box with
partial walls.

☐ Modular Apartment_Guilhem Roustan

© Alejandro Bahamón/Paris, France

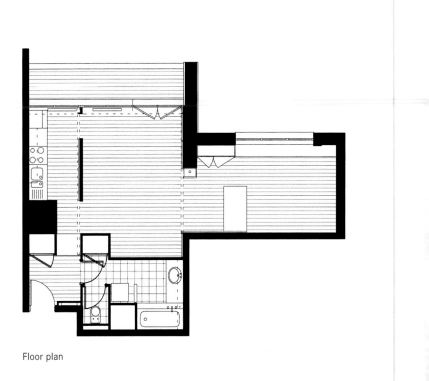

Floor plan

□ The renovation of this apartment
started with a highly efficient
original plan that retained the
advantages of a modern design and
took precise steps to balance the
light and space. The sliding wooden
doors add warmth and make it
possible to completely transform the
space, referring back to the original
plan of the apartment.

☐ The furnishings were kept to a minimum to emphasize the white walls, which reflect the light and provide a background for works of art. Most of the closets are built in, vastly increasing the amount of storage space without filling the apartment with ostentatious furniture.

Duplex Kang_Shichieh Lu/CJ Studio

© Kuomin Lee/Taipei, Taiwan

☐ This project consists of a duplex renovation located on a busy street in Taipei. The elongated and narrow surface area of the space was given a makeover by introducing a frosted glass panel on the rear façade and painting the walls, floors, and ceiling in white to generate continuity, structure, and luminosity.

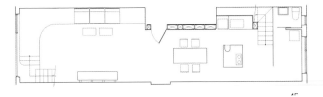

Lower level

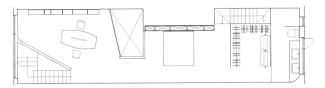

Upper level

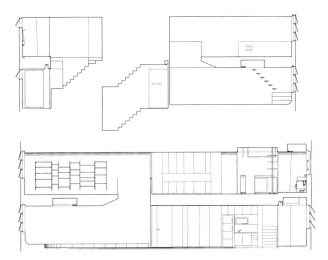

Sections

☐ The double-height space that vertically links the studio and the living area is the nucleus of the residence. The transparency of the staircase connecting the two levels captures and filters natural light in a dynamic way, while the extensive use of white enhances the feeling of open space and weightlessness.

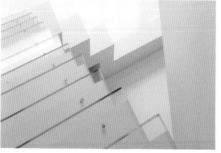

☐ The transparency of the staircase
that connects the two levels
captures and filters natural light in a
dynamic manner, while the extensive
use of white enhances the feeling of
space and weightlessness.

Impossible Thinness_Valerio Dewalt Train Associates

© Barbara Karant/Chicago, IL, United States

235

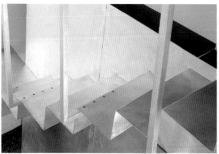

☐ This spectacular Chicago residence is located on the 58th and 59th floors of a Michigan Avenue high-rise dominated by views of the looming John Hancock Center tower to the north. The duplex, once a single space, was divided into "ceremonial" and functional areas, each devised out of a specific material—metal on the first level and wood on the second.

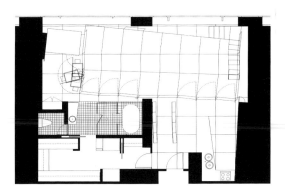

Lower level

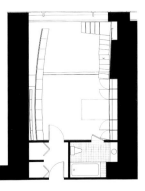

Upper level

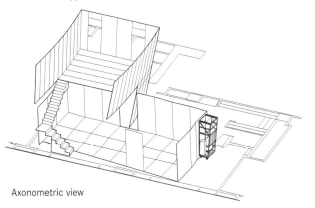

Axonometric view

☐ The threadlike staircase that
leads to the second floor is almost
imperceivable due to its weightless
quality. The studio space is attached
to one of the pivoting metal panels,
where it functions as part of both
the sleeping area and the bathing
area, but can also participate in the
ceremonial space.

□ This residence constitutes a
diaphanous space with an abstract
composition of concept and form.
Steel and wood panels delineate
both the kitchen and the bathroom
areas. The bathroom is enveloped in
mirror and glass, enhancing the
illusion of space.

All Lines_Marco Savorelli

© Matteo Piazza/Milan, Italy

This project entailed the restoration of an attic apartment in the historic center of Milan. The 968-square-foot area was transformed into a modern, sophisticated, and elegant loft-style apartment through the implementation of dark hardwood floors, white walls, and minimalist lines within a single space.

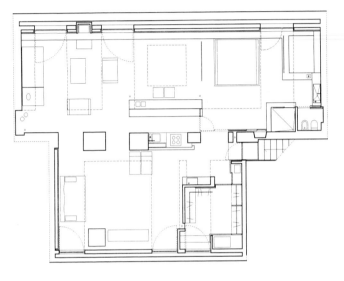

Floor plan

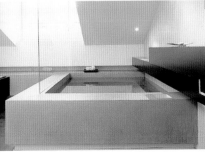

☐ The service areas such as the bathroom, kitchen, and storage were transformed into monolithic volumes that become works of art in and of themselves, given their highly esthetic and visual qualities that also serve to amplify spatial perception.

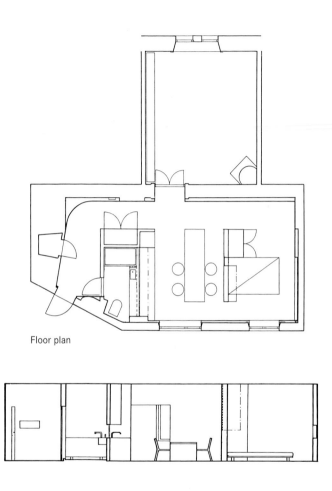

Floor plan

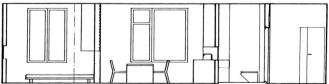

Sections

This private apartment was commissioned by a young businessman who wanted a serene haven from work where he could disconnect and relax. A noticeable emphasis is placed on horizontal lines, expressed through long niches along bare surfaces and the series of cupboards across the living room wall. These lines give the illusion of extended space and lend continuity to the interior design.

Between the kitchen and
bathroom a horizontal acid-etched
glass window acts as a lightbox
when the light is turned on in either
space. The cedarwood bathtub and
basin were custom-designed by the
architects, as were other furnishings
inside the home.

Photographer's Apartment_Tanner Leddy Maytum Stacy Architects

© Stan Musilek, Sharon Reisdorph/San Francisco, CA, United States

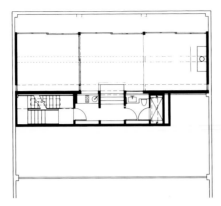

Floor plan

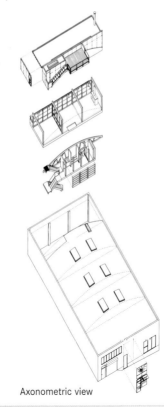

Axonometric view

□ This photographer's apartment is an expansion of an existing industrial structure. Superimposed on the original structure, it enjoys splendid views of the city and bay. Laid out as a series of spaces, the studio is located on the ground floor, followed by a mezzanine and the upper floor, where the living space is located, with the roof serving as an outdoor terrace.

□ A staircase separates the service areas from the main living space, which contains the bedroom, dining room, and living room. The kitchen and the bathroom are situated a half-level below this area, yet remain visually connected to the main space.

Flexible Loft_Page Goolrick

© John M. Hall/New York, NY, United States

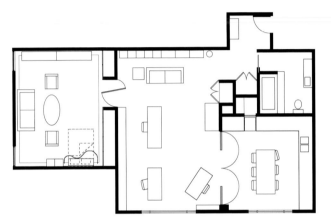

Floor plan

□ This loft functions as a permanent design laboratory where materials, models, and prototypes are incorporated into the apartment's construction details. The flexibility of the furniture and the many ways it can be arranged allow the space to be used as a residence, architectural office, or exhibit space, or for entertaining.

□ The space is organized into three main functions: a central area used as a living room or exhibit space; another area allocated to the kitchen and the meeting space; and finally, the bedroom or most private studio.

West Village Apartment_Desai-Chia Studio

© Joshua McHugh/New York City, NY, United States

The design of this apartment had to be flexible enough to permit entertaining and to accommodate visitors for short periods of time within a minimal space. Grouping the service areas, such as the kitchen, bathroom, and laundry room, on a side wall ensured efficient use of the space while optimizing placement of the fixtures

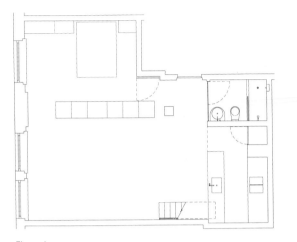

Floor plan

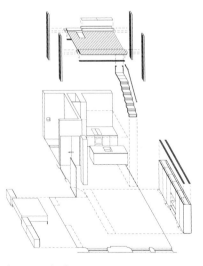

Axonometric view

The bathroom is finished in polished cement and stucco, while the kitchen counter is a single cement slab. A frosted glass door allows natural light to flow into the bathroom while also shedding light into the foyer.

Four Atmospheres in One_Hugh Broughton Architects

© Carlos Domínguez/Gloucestershire, United Kingdom

□ Hugh Broughton Architects managed to preserve this home's classic atmosphere by maintaining the white walls and the wood floor. However, the overall space features new elements that give it a contemporary and functional air. By freeing up the space and adding minimal furnishings, the architect created the desired sensation of amplitude and spatial continuity.

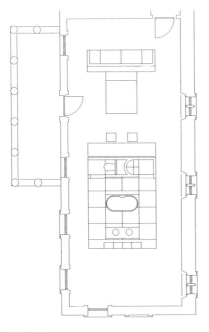

Floor plan

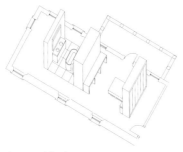

Axonometric view

□ The former dance hall, located at
the southern part of the house, was
divided in the 1920s to create a
series of smaller rooms with low
ceilings. The bathroom zone is
defined by pieces of stone that
contrast with the existing wood
floor, while fixtures and lights built
into the false ceiling reinforce the
project's characteristics and adapt
to functional needs.

☐ Apartment in l'Hospitalet_José Luis López

© Pep Escoda/Barcelona, Spain

☐ This renovated apartment is an open, continuous space in which all the rooms are integrated through the use of furnishings or the architecture itself. A circular sliding door made of wood and parchment isolates the bedroom from the central space, which is composed of the living, dining, and kitchen areas.

☐ Porex, a material that resembles
brick, covers two of the main
walls, providing excellent thermal
insulation and soundproofing,
and adding a touch of warmth to
the interior.

Apartment Veen_Moriko Kira

© Christian Richters / Amsterdam, Netherlands

☐ Originally distributed around a large hall, this residential space was redefined to accommodate a more comfortable and contemporary lifestyle. Doors were removed, moldings were eliminated, and parquet floors were replaced with polished cement.

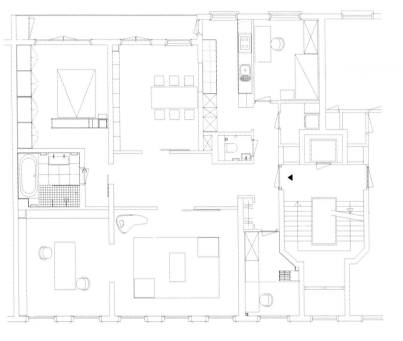

Floor plan

☐ Subtle apertures like this one in the kitchen serve to visually link the different areas in a way that adds to the abstract and geometric nature of the interior design. The extensive use of white creates a luminous and contemporary interior.

☐ Apartment Xiangshan_Hank M. Chao/Mohen Design International

© Moder hou/Shanghai, China

☐ This apartment stands out for its
elegant and timeless Asian-style
interior, characterized by a variety of
textures, materials, and dark tones.
Raw gray granite, stainless steel
sheets, and rusted metals define
the general look of the home and
add a sleek, contemporary edge to
the design.

Floor plan

□ A raw metal wall at the entrance leads to the private interiors, which are separated from the common areas by an interior bamboo garden. The main area features a dining table that seemingly floats off the ground and is supported by a structure concealed at one end.

☐ The illumination employed inside
the interior garden filters through
the screens and produces a glowing
effect that lends drama to the
interior spaces of the residence.

Night and Day_Vicent van Duysen

© Jan Verlinde/Antwerp, Belgium

The object of the design of this
apartment was to use the existing
structure of the two areas that make
up the apartment and instill a more
open and spacious atmosphere.
The day area consists of the living
and dining room and has no formal
entrance, while the night area
is made up of the bedroom and
bathroom, located along a central
corridor that opens completely
through the use of full-length
sliding doors.

□ A long glass wall visually marks
the border between the kitchen and
the living and dining area. The
spacious living room is divided by a
large supporting pillar; a long dining
table and armchair are to its left and
in front of the kitchen, while the
sitting and reading area is situated
comfortably on large rugs and
carpets to its right.

☐ The bathroom area is located along a hallway and can be joined or separated by large sliding doors. The extensive use of white prevents this area from seeming small or cluttered.

Apartment in Margareten_Lichtblau-Wagner Architekten

© Bruno Klomfar/Vienna, Austria

□ The top floor of a building in Vienna's Margareten district was converted into two symmetrical apartments. The architects' goal was to create original, contemporary, functional space without resorting to luxurious finishes and sophisticated details. The absence of interior walls and unnecessary finishes resulted in lower costs and is in keeping with the new interior esthetic.

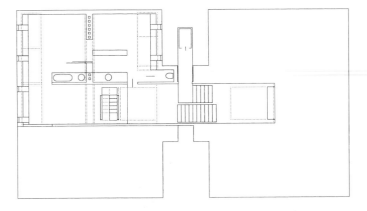

Floor plan (apartment 1)

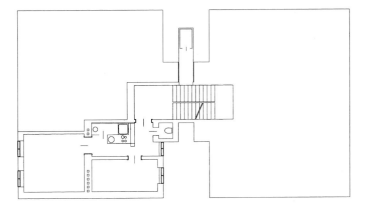

Floor plan (apartment 2)

☐ To compensate for the small size of the apartments, a common area, placed next to the stairs, is used for storage, as a laundry room, or to expand the social area as needed.

Retro Chic_UdA – Ufficio di Architettura

© Heiko Semeyer/Nice, France

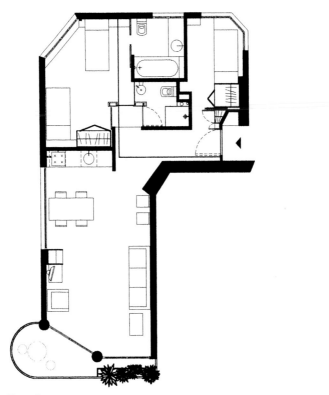

Floor plan

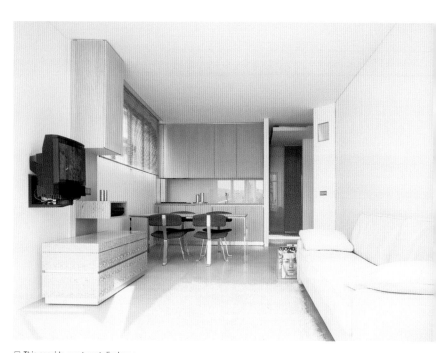

☐ This seaside apartment displays a very urban-chic style within a relatively small space, using lighting and storage techniques that keep it clean and tidy. At the entrance, a short corridor leads to a small room on the right in which large closets are concealed behind wood panels. The capacious living room shares the same space as the kitchen and dining area.

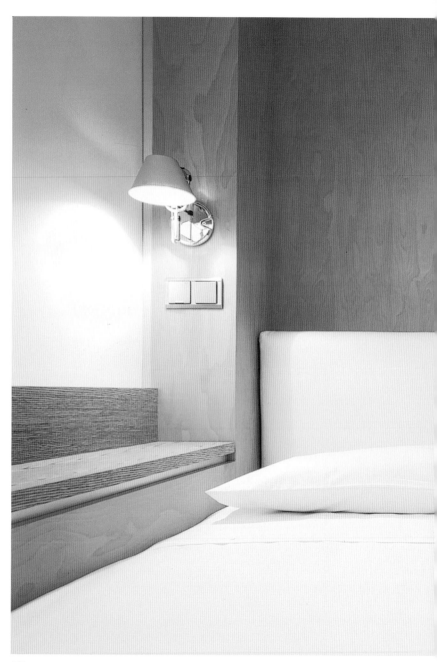

Lords Telephone Exchange_Paskin Kyriakides Sands Architects

© Paskin Kyriakides Sands Architects/London, United Kingdom

□ The original structure of this building was ideal for creating urban living spaces on multiple levels, resulting in the creation of a series of unique, modern apartments with fine details and finishes organized within a plan that made the most of the structural and lighting conditions that already existed.

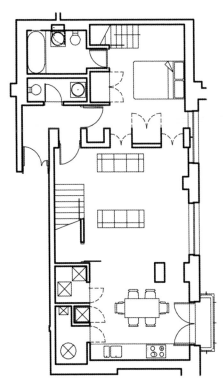

Floor plan

Elevations

☐ Islington Apartment_Caruso-St. John Architects

© Hélène Binet/London, United Kingdom

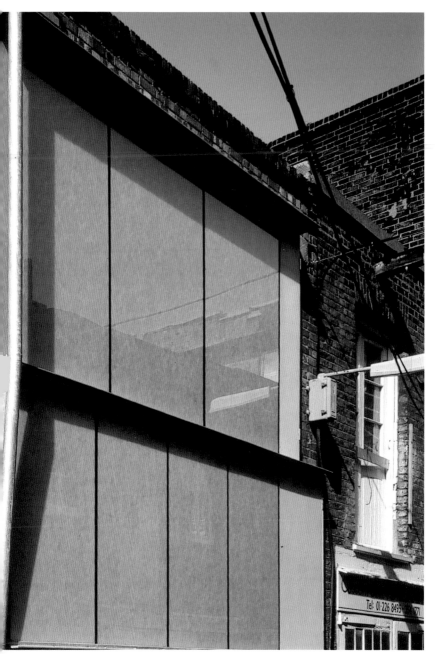

Tel: 01-226 8495

□ This house and studio are located in the neighborhood of Islington, in the northern part of London. The project's goal was to create a space in which the existing elements merge with the new ones in the same formal language. The architects employed modest materials like chipboard panels of plaster and cement fiber, and insulating glass.

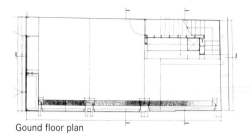

Gound floor plan

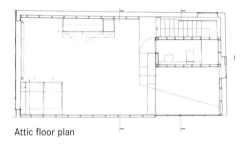

Attic floor plan

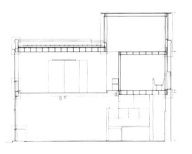

Section

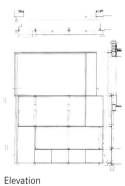

Elevation

□ Playful and Intimate_Gary Chang/Edge Design Institute

© Almond Chu/Hong Kong, China

☐ This apartment, located on the east island of Hong Kong, was designed by Gary Chang as his personal residence. The goal of the project was to create a space that, despite its reduced proportions, contains all the necessary residential functions, yet has flexibility for rest and leisure.

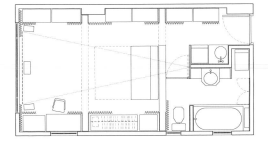

Floor plan

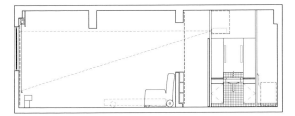

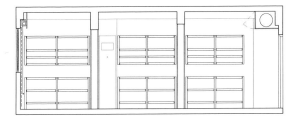

Longitudinal sections

☐ In order to make the most of the principal window located in the back part of the residence, the architect grouped the bathroom, kitchen, and laundry room in the front. Thus, the main space enjoys the window, which is the best source of natural light. As an empty space, this area could also accommodate diverse functions such as the bedroom, living room, study, and video room.

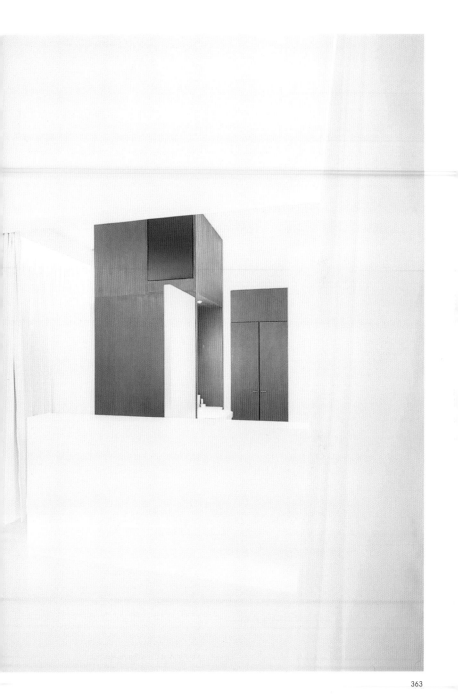

Apartment on Baró de la Barre_Araceli Manzano, Esther Flavià

© Eugeni Pons/Barcelona, Spain

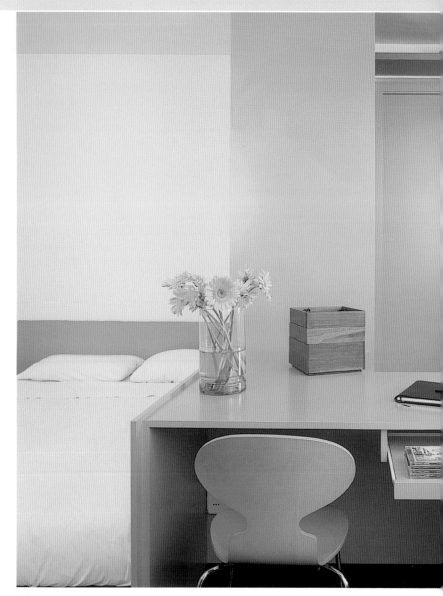

□ Warm, cozy areas were created inside this 540-square-foot space by taking advantage of the abundant natural light. Highly functional furniture with simple lines ensures efficient use of the space. The living room, dining room, kitchen, and bedroom share a single space, while the bathroom and dressing room are the only areas that are completely closed off.

Floor plan

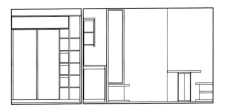

Sections

Apartment in Shepherd's Bush_ Jeremy King

© Montse Garriga/London, United Kingdom

□ The plan for renovating this apartment involved creating an efficient home and workspace for one person within the confines of this small area, while providing for the maximum possible amount of storage. A long storage unit was hung on the side wall and contains closet space as well as a drawing table and office area, which can be folded away when not in use.

☐ Two doors in the storage unit become a worktable that folds away at night. The purity of the space was maintained by anchoring the unit to the wall while leaving open areas above and below it.

Studio in Covent Garden_René Dekker

© James Silverman/London, United Kingdom

This small space, located in an industrial area of Covent Garden, was transformed into an office and residence for the owner. Neutral colors and functional furniture lend a tranquil and comfortable atmosphere, characterized by the owner's taste for Asian elements and decorative objects.

☐ Simple lines and plenty of storage space allow this small residence to feel spacious and comfortable. The bedroom contains of a foldout bed and serves as a dining room during the day, when the bed is stored away. The wall unit conceals various closets, which can be used for storage space, avoiding any sensation of clutter within the home.

Floor plan

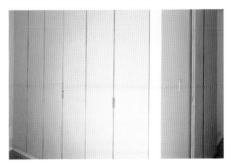

☐ The refurbishment of this one-bedroom apartment involved the creation of a work area, a change in the layout of the kitchen, and the modification of some partitions. The walls were replaced by mobile panels to provide fluidity, as well as to gain luminosity and views of the exterior.

Apartment in Andorra_Elisabet Faura, Gerard Veciana

© Eugeni Pons/Andorra la Vella, Andorra

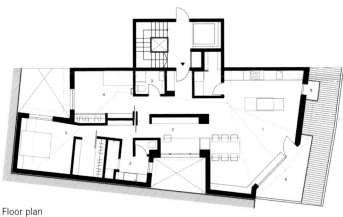

Floor plan

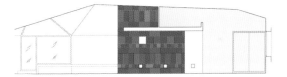

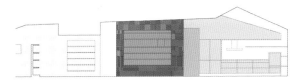

Sections

□ One of the main objectives of this
project was to achieve maximum
clarity, given the lack of open views
available within the apartment.
The living area is presided over by
the kitchen and dining area that look
out through a full-height glass wall.
The entrance wall articulates the
circulation pattern and incorporates
a library and office space.

□ A series of partitions were introduced to direct natural light throughout the various interior spaces, creating a dynamic relationship with materials such as concrete, resin, parquet, slate, and wengue and the colors green, red, and black.

Strand Dwelling_Satellite Design Workshop

© Thomas Haywood/London, United Kingdom

☐ The top two floors of this building
in the heart of London were
converted into an open-plan home
with the maximum degree of
flexibility and making use of all the
natural light entering through the
roof. The limited palette of materials
consists mainly of tinted oak
flooring, a concrete shell for the
kitchen and a rusted-metal effect for
the stairs and rafters.

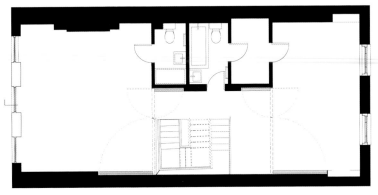

Ground floor

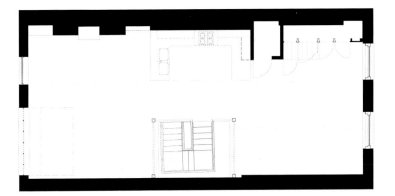

First floor

Apartment in Medellín_Guillermo Arias

© Carlos Tobón/Medellín, Colombia

☐ Designed for a couple, this apartment is located within a new building in the hilly neighborhood of Medellín, Colombia. Determined by the original characteristics of the space, the design aims to liberate the interior of walls and partitions and establish a greater connection between the two existing terraces. A comfortable space was integrated into the smaller terrace as a tranquil place from which to contemplate the bamboo forest.

Floor plan

□ The interior spaces are clearly geared toward the exterior in order to take advantage of the relaxing and breathtaking views of the forest. The furnishings are both comfortable and stylish, suitable for a contemporary and practical lifestyle.

Walking on Air_UdA – Ufficio di Architettura

© Emilio Conti/Turin, Italy

☐ The commission was to remodel a dark, empty attic on the fourth floor of an eighteenth-century building in the baroque center of Turin, Italy. The staircase joining the two levels increases the flow of natural light as a result of its transparency, transforming it into an ethereal element that does not interrupt the fluidity of the space.

☐ The staircase leads to the upper
level, which contains the kitchen,
dining room, and living room.
Floating planes of glass generate a
continued sensation of
weightlessness and luminosity.

Gallery & Apartment_Marco Piono

© Werner Huthmacher/Berlin, Germany

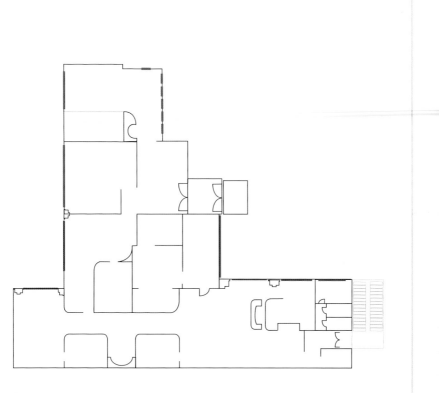

Floor plan

☐ This 4,300-square-foot space,
formerly part of a factory, was
designed and decorated by its
owner, an Italian painter and
sculptor. The residence also
functions as a gallery and atelier.

Loft in Tribeca_Roger Hirsch, Myriam Corti, Tocar Interior Design

© Michael Moran/New York, NY, United States

☐ The first step in renovating this loft was to eliminate as many interior walls as possible in order to create a greater feeling of space and light. Light and flexible materials and design elements were used to fulfill the requirements of the project while preserving the proportions of the space that had been created. The guest room, for example, consists of a foldout bed and two curtains that define the space.

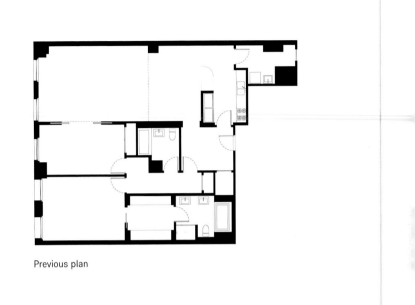

Previous plan

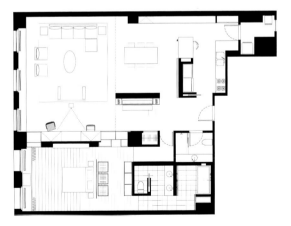

New plan

□ Apartment on the Coast_Joan Estrada

© Nuria Fuentes/Barcelona, Spain

□ The goal of this project was to convert an old shop on the ground floor of a building into a residence. The two existing façades were completely opened up with large windows that not only allow light into the interior, but also link it with the exterior.

□ Sliding glass doors separating the centrally located bedrooms and bathroom allow light to enter and fully integrate them with the rest of the house.

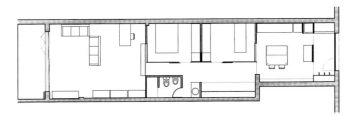

Floor plan

☐ Horizontal Unit_Stephen Quinn & Elise Ovanessoff

© Jordi Miralles/London, United Kingdom

☐ The finished interior of this small
loft still has traces of the original
Georgian house built 200 years ago.
Nevertheless, the architects have
managed to create a completely
modern apartment with comfortable
and practical surroundings through
the use of space and light combined
with the existing high ceilings.

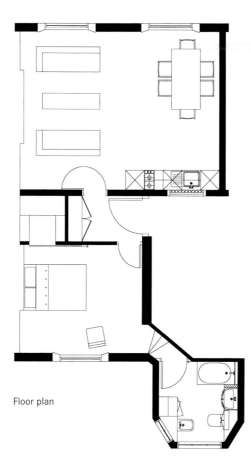

Floor plan

Apartment in Bucharest_Westfourth Architecture

© Mihail Moldoveanu/Bucharest, Romania

☐ This apartment is arranged around the central corridor, which serves as a reference point for the placement of all the other elements. While the structure made it impossible to open up the interior entirely, the apartment is nevertheless characterized by continuous, flowing space.

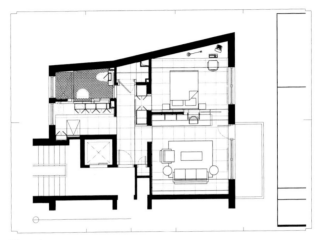

Floor plan

☐ The clean lines and restraint
evident in the main rooms are
also reflected in the kitchen
and bathroom. Small openings to
the building's central courtyard
provide natural lighting and
ventilation.

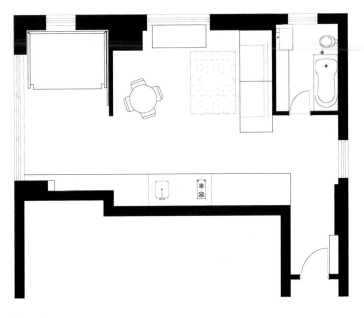

Floor plan

□ This project consists of a small studio inside a 1920s building in Sydney that was transformed into a comfortable one-bedroom apartment. An artistic wall created by Tim Richardson was introduced, providing the option to separate or join the bedroom and the living area. The architects preserved the original bathroom tiles, creating a greater visual impact.

Jordi and Aída Residence_ Josep Llobet

© Eugeni Pons/Girona, Spain

☐ After enduring various transformations and refurbishments, this apartment was gutted and reorganized in order to adapt it to a more contemporary lifestyle. The new interior consists of an open, fluid space that establishes the different environments through furnishings and materials.

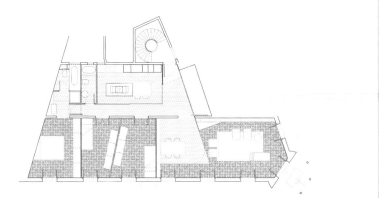

Floor plan

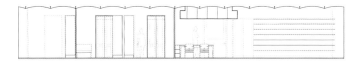

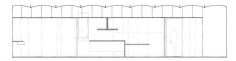

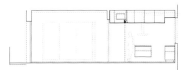

Sections

☐ The kitchen, contained within
sliding glass panels, occupies the
nucleus of the apartment, alongside
the entrance, and features a large
island designed by the architect,
which can be used either as a
cooking counter or as an informal
dining table.

☐ The original mosaic flooring in the living area, windows, and vaulted ceilings lend this apartment an authentic and casual atmosphere that offers an alternative to hard-edged minimalist design. Practical furnishings such as the kitchen modules, dining table, closets, and shelves were designed by the architect.

Steve Apartment_Marco Savorelli

© Matteo Piazza/Milan, Italy

□ The complete refurbishment of
this apartment entailed the
elimination of all interior partitions
and the creation of an interior
composed of three main spaces. The
doors were replaced by sliding full-
length panels that seamlessly join
with the walls when closed, and the
lacquered wood furnishings were
specially designed by the architect.

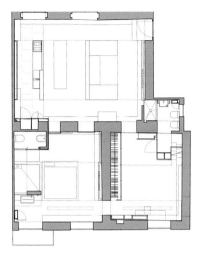

Floor plan

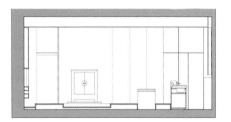

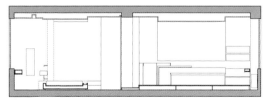

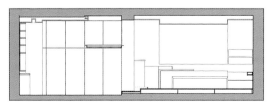

Sections

⊐ The living area, dining area, and
kitchen—which is discreetly
concealed behind a half-height
partition—occupy the central area of
the apartment. The design was
based on feng shui principles in
order to achieve a balanced and
harmonious atmosphere within a
contemporary framework.

Hermosilla 18_Ignacio Vicens, José Antonio Ramos

© Eugeni Pons/Madrid, Spain

☐ This penthouse apartment situated within a new building stands out for its expansively high ceilings, double-height volumes, and interconnected interior spaces.

Type plan

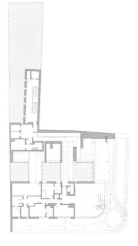

Penthouse floor plan

□ A balcony wraps around the main living area, which incorporates a curved wall that adds movement and character to the architecture.

☐ **East Meets West**_Tow Studios

© Björg/New York, NY, United States

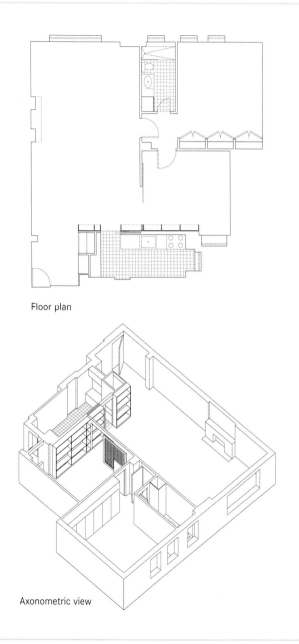

Floor plan

Axonometric view

□ Situated on the ninth floor and surrounded by views of Central Park, this apartment's only reminder of its location in a congested metropolis is a peripheral view of the Fifth Avenue skyline. The layout of the space is arranged much like a loft, separated into rooms by means of sliding doors and panels in translucent glass and painted wood.

☐ In the kitchen, standard beech
cabinets and a stainless steel sink
provide a functional and modern
cooking space. The master bath is
finished in French limestone, and
the frameless walk-in glass shower
offers a view of the city. Flush
mirrored medicine cabinets
conceal toiletries and other
products, reflecting the views
into the bathroom.

☐ Pink House_Filippo Bombace

© Luigi Filetici/Rome, Italy

☐ Situated inside a mansion dating back to 1950, this apartment was renovated based on its original structure, which presented an irregular geometric plan. Simple design solutions were integrated into the space, using differences in ceiling heights, transparent materials, and the distribution of furnishings to differentiate the spaces, add color, and highlight the original floor plan of the apartment.

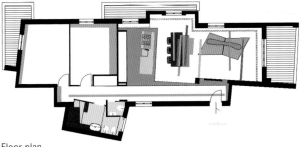

Floor plan

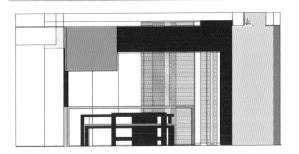

Section

Sampaoli House_Claudio Caramel

© Paolo Utimpergher/Padua, Italy

□ Created inside an old print shop, formerly used as a carpentry warehouse, this residence is located in the center of Padua, in northern Italy. The private spaces are defined by independent bedrooms, but the area that dominates the interior is a large room that groups the functions of the living room, dining room, and kitchen.

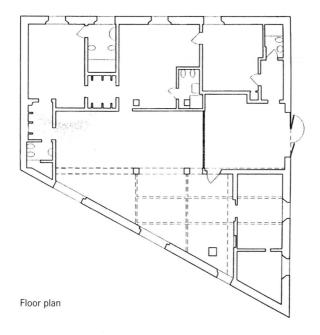

Floor plan

Formal Unity_Guillermo Arias, Luis Cuartas

© E. Consuegra, P. Rojas/Bogotá, Colombia

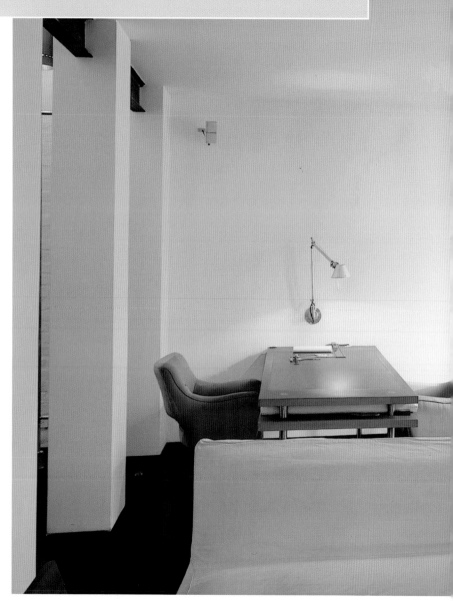

☐ This apartment occupies a large part of what was once a traditional residence in a building in Bogotá that dates back to the 1930s. Since the apartment is located on the top floor of the building, the architect envisioned a plan that would modify the roof in various ways in order to enrich the space by responding to the different lines of sight.

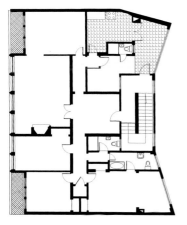

Previous floor plan

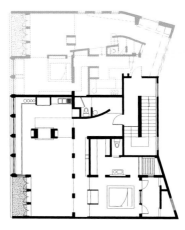

Present floor plan

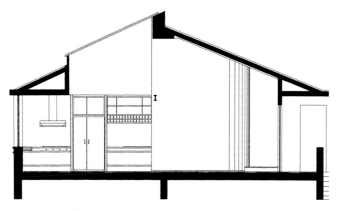

Transversal section

Small Loft in Vienna_Lakonis Architekten

© Margherita Spiluttini/Vienna, Austria

☐ This interior, originally a six-room apartment in the center of Vienna, was converted into an open loft-style space for living and working. All the interior walls were demolished and the divisions between the bathroom, the kitchen, and the bedroom were created along a single, red wall.

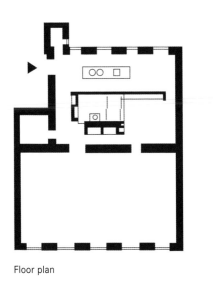

Floor plan

☐ Apartment in Plaza Mayor_Manuel Ocaña del Valle

© Alfonso Postigo/Madrid, Spain

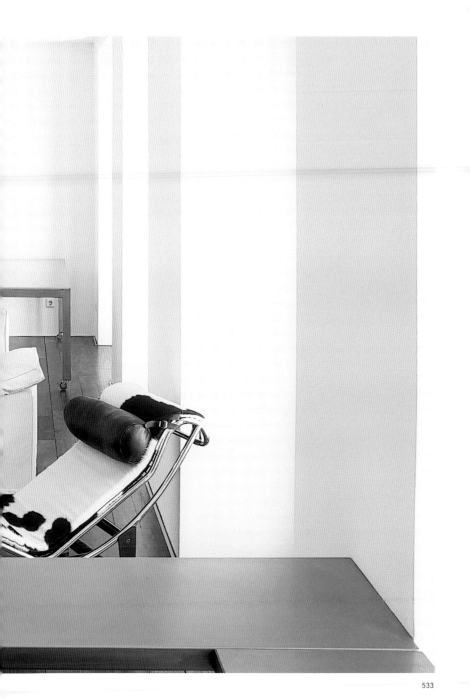

□ The architect of this residence restructured the original space by creating a regular and orthogonal order. The new distribution divides the loft into two large zones: an open area for the primary living space and another, with similar dimensions, that was broken down into smaller areas.

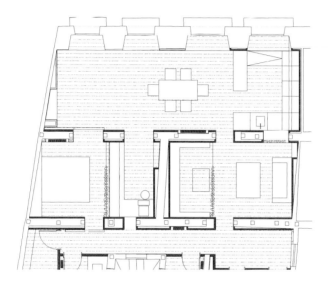

Floor plan

☐ The stainless steel table, which serves as a counter in the kitchen and as an informal dining room table, is a folding sheet attached to the wall, which maintains continuity. The full-length windows take advantage of natural light to illuminate the areas in the rear of the apartment.

☐ The interior of this building was previously run-down, and was divided by a confusing and disorganized series of exposed beams. Its transformation into a single space with diverse functions was resolved by creating different areas that relate to one another and define the functions of the residence.

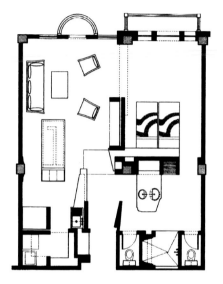

Floor plan

Apartment in Casa Magarola_J. S. Ràfols (building renovation),
© Montse Garriga/Barcelona, Spain B. Salas (design)

☐ Formerly part of a nineteenth-
century seminary in Barcelona's old
quarter, this space was converted
into a broad, well-lit, and peaceful
apartment. The interior designer
took full advantage of the building's
unique features, very similar to
those of a typical loft, without
adopting the minimalist approach
often seen in these types of homes.

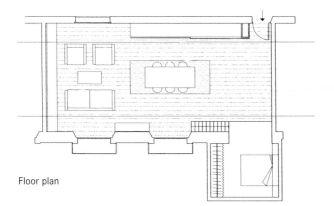

Floor plan

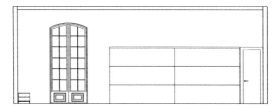

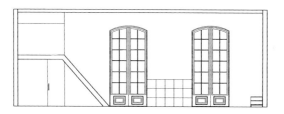

Sections

☐ At one end of the apartment, the
designer took advantage of the high
ceilings in order to place the
bathroom below the bedroom. The
sheet metal used in constructing
the loft, a decorative touch in and
of itself, was left exposed.

Romantic Apartment_Peter Tyberghien

© Alejandro Bahamón/Paris, France

□ This apartment is located in Paris's 9th Arrondissement, close to Montmartre and minutes from the center of the city. Although small spaces are the rule in large European capitals, this interior has unusual features for an apartment of this type, including natural light and ventilation.

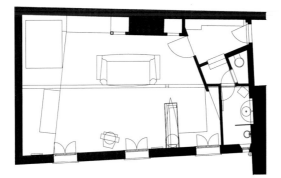

Floor plan

☐ The warm materials, such as
wood and natural fibers, contrast
with the austere lines and decorative
objects to create a comfortable,
peaceful atmosphere. The metal
beam running across the interior
was used to divide the space into
two long halves and supports a
series of track lights that supply
most of the artificial illumination.

☐ Apartment in Janelas Verdes_João Maria Ventura

© Sergio Mah/Lisbon, Portugal

The objective of this low-budget project was to turn a two-story space into a comfortable home for a single person. The upper level, which contains the entrance, was transformed into a long, narrow living room that opens onto a courtyard at one end. The lower floor houses the bedroom, a laundry room underneath the stairs, and an exit to the courtyard.

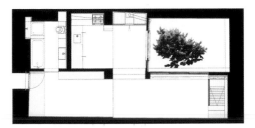

Main floor plan

Lower floor plan

Longitudinal section

Transversal section

☐ This small space seems larger due to the presence of the courtyard, the generous use of white, and the large windows that communicate with the exterior. The small corridor also doubles as a sitting area.

□ This project is an original proposal that provides a spacious residence within 270 square feet through the implementation of a hydraulic and electrical system. This technology was applied to the various furnishings within the space, allowing it to be transformed from bedroom and living room into dining area and kitchen.

Floor plans

□ Various elements can be concealed underneath the floor, including the bed, bathtub, and chairs. The hydraulic system also regulates the height of the furnishings, while the electrical system moderates the lighting to the required intensity.

Monolocal_Studio Associato Bettinelli

© Andrea Martiradonna/Milan, Italy

Floor plan

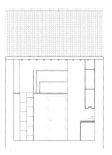

Sections

☐ The reduced surface area of this apartment was optimized by distributing the living space on two levels. All the areas except for the bathroom remain open in order to maintain fluidity throughout, and the use of white tones lends the apartment a greater sense of amplitude.

☐ The bedroom was situated on the upper level and fitted with closets for optimum storage space. Carefully planned illumination features two skylights that shed natural light throughout the entire space and contemporary light fixtures embedded into the walls for a clean, minimalist look.

Dwelling in Barcelona_Nacho Marta

© Jose Luis Hausmann/Barcelona, Spain

□ The refurbishment of this apartment mainly involved eliminating as many walls and doors as possible—the kitchen and bathroom are the only areas that can be closed off—in order to create a greater sense of space. The original arch and pillars were retained to visually distinguish the lounge from the bedroom.

☐ In the bedroom, a sliding door separates the bathroom from the closet, thus respecting the need for privacy while also ensuring that clothes, shoes, and other personal objects are out of sight. Small spaces do not allow for much furniture, but as a result they tend to present storage problems. Built-in closets or sliding doors are often the best solution.

Small Apartment_Manel Torres/In Disseny, Jorge Rangel

© Stephan Zahring/Caldes de Montbui, Spain

□ This apartment was conceived as a single, open space characterized by its fluid lines and the absence of visual barriers. Only the bedroom remains separated from the main space by a sliding door that controls the entry of light and the relationship with the surrounding areas.

☐ A large sofa and glass coffee
table create a simple yet
comfortable living area from which
the entire loft can be appreciated.
The roller blinds filter the light
flowing through the windows.

Apartment in New York_Morris Sato Studio

© Michael Moran/New York, NY, United States

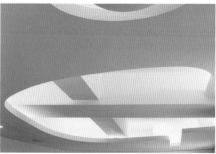

A curved partition transforms this small space into a comfortable and dynamic residence. Undoubtedly, the most interesting feature of this apartment is the ceiling, which partially exposes the original structure of the building through an oval-shaped composition of foam panels, and integrates an indirect lighting system that produces an abstract, futuristic effect.

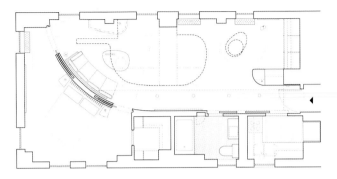

Floor plan

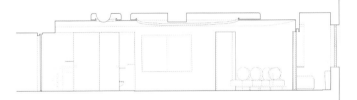

Longitudinal section

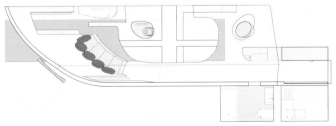

Projection

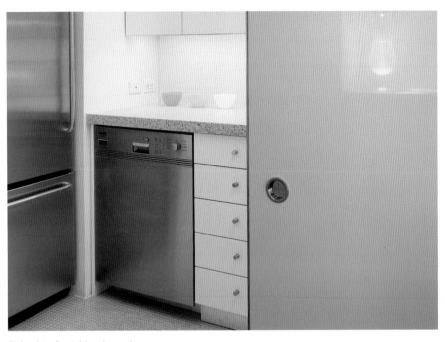

☐ A variety of materials, colors, and
furniture designed by the architect
compose an interior characterized
by cool, elegant tones and a
minimalist esthetic.

Slender_Deadline Design

© Ludger Paffrath/Berlin, Germany

☐ The architects who built this unique apartment atop a narrow building in the historic center of Berlin were challenged with a reduced 62- x 16-foot area. The residence was conceived as a series of functional spaces that flow into one another and culminate in a cantilevered structure that accommodates the bedroom.

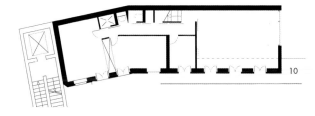

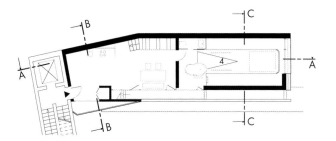

Floor plans

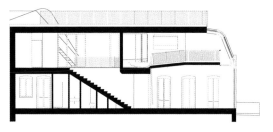

Section

☐ Simple materials such as
exposed and painted concrete
emphasize the qualities and
constructive elements of the space.
Natural light floods the interiors
through the large, full-length
windows and successive skylights.

☐ Sober materials and forms
contrast with decorative details and
accessories like the romantic-style
mirror in the bathroom.

Light on Dark_Eva Prats & Ricardo Flores

© Eugeni Pons/Barcelona, Spain

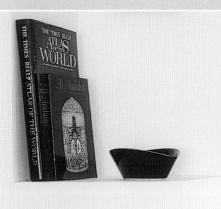

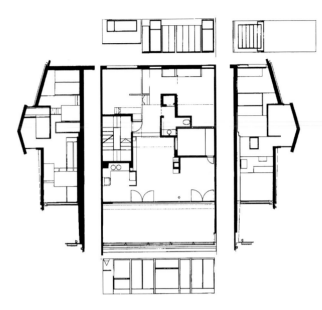

Floor plan and sections

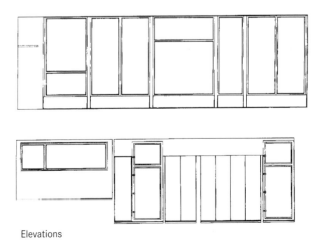

Elevations

□ This young couple's flat occupies the former attic of a single-family house located in Sarrià, an area of central Barcelona. The space was conceived as open plan; the only enclosed area is the bathroom unit, around which all other household activities revolve. The closet in the kitchen serves as a pantry while also forming a visual barrier between the living and eating areas.

□ This practical apartment consists of a living room linked to the dining area, one bedroom, one bathroom, a kitchen, and a studio. The principal feature is the living/dining room that can be transformed into two spaces by sliding doors. The resulting smaller room includes a corner desk, as well as a sofa bed, allowing the area to be used as a guest bedroom.

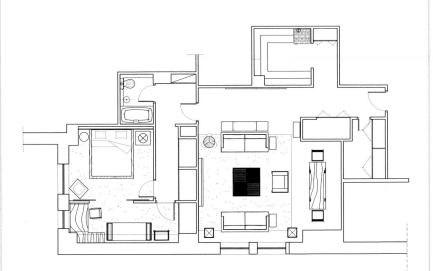

Floor plan

Turning Torso Apartment_Samark Arkitektur & Design

© James Silverman/Malmö, Sweden

☐ Situated inside the Turning Torso
apartment building designed by
Santiago Calatrava, this apartment
looks out over the bay in Malmö,
Sweden. Conceived as a continuous,
open space, the tall ceilings and
panoramic views create an
extraordinary sense of
expansiveness emphasized by the
decoration and materials employed.

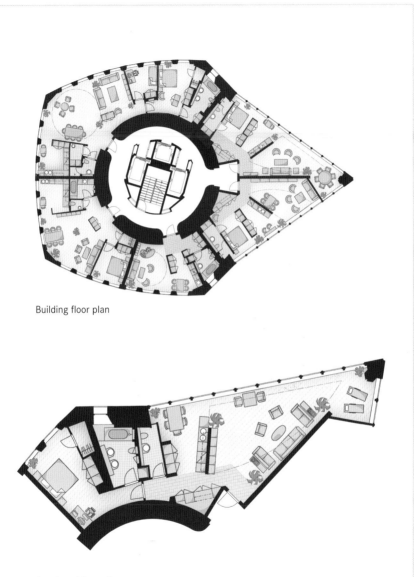

Building floor plan

Apartment floor plan

☐ The limestone used for the floors and the white tones used along the walls and ceiling create a cool yet intimate atmosphere, while the inclination of the windows lends movement and character to the interior design.

☐ The interior designers aimed for a luxurious atmosphere that would also be functional and practical to live in. A restrained color palette, comfortable furnishings, and quality materials characterize this apartment in Malmö.